South Dakota Fish Species

Game Fish & Panfish

Billy Grinslott & Kinsey Marie Books

ISBN - 9781965098875

Creek Chubs and Golden Shiners are two types of minnows that are considered panfish. There are several types of shiners. Many people will use them as bate to catch larger fish. Creek chubs are silver in color and golden shiner have a gold color. There are also many types of silver shiners.

Redear sunfish are known for their red or orange-edged gill flaps. They are a type of sunfish that thrive in warm, quiet waters, feeding primarily on mollusks and snails, and can grow up to 12 inches and weigh as much as 2 pounds. They are also known as shellcracker, due to their diet and the way they crush shells. The redear sunfish will thrive in most warm-water lakes and streams.

Longear sunfish are small, thin-bodied fish with a unique long ear flap on their gill cover, that how they got their name long ear. They are often mistaken for a pumpkinseed. They have an olive to rusty-brown back, a bright orange belly. They typically reach a length of 4.5 inches. They are mostly active during the day and inactive at night.

The Green Sunfish is blue green in color. It has yellow flecks on both its scales and some parts of its sides. The Green Sunfish also has broken blue stripes which is why some people confuse it with the Bluegill. Green Sunfish are very adaptable, they can live in any body of water that has vegetation or weeds. Green sunfish are opportunistic feeders, consuming insects, small fish, and other invertebrates.

Orange spotted sunfish are mostly found in floodplains of the United States of the Great Lakes. Its beautiful shiny silvery-blue body has reddish-orange spots, which give it its name, orange spotted sunfish. They are usually found in southern Muunesota but are too small to be popular with anglers. Their average length is 3 inches. They are a small fish.

The Warmouth is a member of the Rock Bass, Green Sunfish and Bluegill family. They can survive in low oxygen environments while other fish cannot. Warmouth can thrive in muddy water, when other fish can't. Warmouth are often confused with rock bass. The difference between the two is in the anal fin: warmouth have three spines on the anal fin ray and rock bass have six spines.

The bluegill also considered a sunfish is the most popular fish to fish for. They are called pan fish because they are about the size of a frying pan. Bluegills love to eat insects and bugs. They have good vision and rely on their keen eyesight to feed. Three types in this group are the Bluegill, Sunfish, and Pumpkinseed.

The Pumpkinseed is also known as pond perch, sun perch, and punky's sunfish. It can be found in numerous lakes, ponds, and rivers. It is their body shape resembling the seed of a pumpkin, that inspired their name. Pumpkinseed sunfish have speckles on their orangish colored sides and back, with a yellow to orange belly and chest. They are active during the day and rest at night near the bottom or in shelter areas.

The Rock Bass is not actually a bass but a member of the sunfish family. The biggest Rock Bass ever caught on record weighs about three pounds and was a little over one foot long. Rock bass prefer waters with rocky vegetated areas, that's how they got their name.

The two most famous perches are the common perch and the yellow perch. The yellow perch has a brilliant greenish yellow color with orange fins. The yellow perch is the biggest one and can grow to a size of 18 inches. It's also known as the jumbo perch. The other type of perch is the white perch. The largest yellow perch ever recorded in South Dakota weighed 2 pounds, 13 ounces.

There are two main types of crappies. The white crappie and the black crappie. They are also members of the sunfish family. The difference between the white and black crappie is one has dark spots and the other has dark lines and is lighter in color. The white crappie has six dorsal fin spines, whereas the black crappie has eight dorsal fin spines. The white crappie can grow bigger and more of the bigger white crappie are caught in North America.

The White sucker fish has the same mouth as a carp. They got their name because their mouth is like a suction cup. They normally are bottom feeders and suck their food from the bottom of the lake. Many people use sucker fish to fish for northern pike and other big game fish. The largest sucker fish, a Blue Sucker caught in South Dakota weighed 12 pounds 7 ounces.

Flathead Catfish, their body is wide but flattened and very low in height. Both eyes are on the top of the flattened head, giving excellent vision to see upward. Flathead catfish live mainly in large bodies of water like big rivers and reservoirs. They prefer deep pools. The South Dakota state record for a flathead catfish is a 67-pound, 8-ounces, Length 51.5 inches.

The black bullhead and yellow bullhead are part of the catfish family. They usually only grow to about 10 inches long. They use their whiskers to help find food. The bullhead is the most common member of the catfish family. Bullheads live in the water containing low oxygen levels. They can survive on low oxygen areas, where other fish can't.

There are several species of catfish. The Channel Catfish are the most fished catfish species with around 8 million anglers fishing for them per year. Channel Catfish have very few teeth and swallow their food whole. Channel catfish live in freshwater rivers, lakes, streams, and ponds. Catfish can live in low oxygen water, like bullheads. The South Dakota state record for a channel catfish is 56 pounds.

Bowfins also known as mudfish or dogfish, can breathe both air and water, putting them at an advantage in low-oxygen waters. Bowfins are often described as prehistoric relics. This is because species can be traced to fossils from the Cretaceous, Eocene and Jurassic period. The largest bowfin caught in South Dakota weighed 8 pounds.

White Bass range in color from a silvery white to a pale green. Their backs are mostly black, while their sides and belly are pale with stripes running along them. White Bass are related to Striped Bass and called wipers. The South Dakota state record for a white bass is 4.70 pounds.

There are few different species of Gar, the Longnose and shortnose gar, and Alligator gar. The Long Nose Gar got its name because of its long mouth that looks like an alligator's mouth. The alligator gar is one of the biggest freshwater fish growing up to 10 feet long. The world record for a catch was set at 327 pounds. The largest gar caught in South Dakota was a longnose gar weighing 20 pounds and measured 52 inches.

Lake Sturgeons have sharp spines on their back, so be careful when handling them. Instead of scales, sturgeon skin is covered in bony plates called scutes, which can be very sharp on young sturgeon. Sturgeons have been around since the dinosaur days. Sturgeons mostly live in large, freshwater lakes and rivers. Their average lifespan is 50 to 60 years. The largest sturgeon caught in South Dakota, a pallid sturgeon, weighed 28.8 pounds.

Shovelnose Sturgeons have sharp spines on their back, so be careful when handling them. Instead of scales, sturgeon skin is covered in bony plates called scutes, which can be very sharp on young sturgeon. Sturgeons have been around since the dinosaur days. Sturgeons mostly live in large, freshwater lakes and rivers. Their average lifespan is 50 to 60 years. The South Dakota record for a shovelnose sturgeon is 6 pounds, 10 ounces.

Male freshwater drum make a rumbling or grunting sound by contracting muscles along their air bladder walls. They have large, ivory-like ear bones that can be up to an inch in diameter, which Native Americans used as necklaces or bracelets and sometimes referred to as the lucky stones. Freshwater drum are primarily bottom feeders, spending much of their time near the bottom of lakes and rivers in search of food. The largest freshwater drum caught in South Dakota weighed 36 pounds and 8 ounces.

The burbot, also known as the eel pout. They get their name because they have a serpent-like or eel-like body. They can wrap their tail around things. There's nothing to worry about if you catch one, they may try to wrap their tail around your arm, but they are harmless. Burbots are adapted to cold water and are found in large, cold rivers, lakes, and reservoirs, primarily preferring freshwater habitats. Burbots are also known as eelpout, lingcod, and lawyer. The largest burbot caught in South Dakota, and current state record, weighed 12 pounds, 7 ounces, Length 33 3/4 inches.

Buffalo Fish are sometimes confused with carp. Buffalo fish have a downward-facing mouth, capable of sucking bits of food out of the silt and sand on the bottom. They have broad bodies, blunt heads, and silvery gray or brown scales. Buffalo fish are members of the suckerfish family. The largest buffalo fish caught in South Dakota, a 50-pound, 15-ounce smallmouth buffalo.

Carp have long been an important food fish to humans. Carp are bottom feeders for the most part and their mouth is made like a suction cup, so they can suck food off the bottom. Carp are good for a lake because they help clean the bottom of the lake. The largest carp caught in South Dakota, a bighead carp, weighed 90 pounds.

The lake trout is one of the biggest of the trout family. The biggest lake trout caught was 72 pounds. Lake trout like to live in lakes that are deep. They like being in the cool water in the deep parts of a lake. They have been reported to live up to 70 years in some Canadian lakes. The largest lake trout caught in South Dakota was a 30-pound fish.

Brook trout are characterized by their olive-green bodies with pale, worm-like markings, red spots with bluish halos, and orange-red fins with white and black edges. They can grow up to 12 inches in length. Brook trout are cold-water fish that prefer clean, clear, and cold streams, lakes, and ponds. The largest brook trout caught in South Dakota weighed 12 pounds.

The rainbow trout gets its name because of its brilliant colors. Rainbow trout populations are good indicators of water pollution because they can only survive in clean waters. They like to live in rivers and streams. Rainbow trout rank among the top five most sought game fish in North America. The South Dakota state record for a rainbow trout is 19 pounds, 4 ounces.

Brown trout can live up to 20 years. Brown trout have higher tolerance for warmer waters than either brook or rainbow trout. Brown trout can be found on almost every continent except Antarctica, and many can be found living in the ocean. The largest brown trout caught in South Dakota, weighed 24 pounds, 8 ounces.

Chinook also known as the king salmon are the most widespread Salmon in North America. Chinook salmon are hatch in freshwater streams and rivers then migrate out to the saltwater environment of the ocean to feed and grow. Chinook salmon are the largest of the Pacific Ocean salmon, that's how they got the name king salmon. The largest Chinook salmon caught in South Dakota, weighed 31.55 pounds. The fish was 36 inches long.

Smallmouth bass have a smaller mouth than the largemouth bass. They also have different markings and are lighter in color. They don't live in most lakes because they prefer living in colder water. They are typically found in the northern states in America because the water is cooler. The current world record smallmouth is an 11-pound, 15-ounce fish caught in Dale Hollow Lake. The largest smallmouth bass ever caught in South Dakota weighed 7 pounds, 4.7 ounces, measured 20.75 inches long.

The largemouth bass is the most sought-after bass in North America. Largemouth bass live in just about every lake in North America. They have great hearing and can hear a crayfish crawling on the bottom of the lake. The current South Dakota state record for a largemouth bass, weighed 9 pounds, 5 ounces, measured 23 inches long.

The sauger is part of the walleye family. There are 2 different types of saugers. The normal sauger and the suageye. The saugeye is a mix of the sauger and walleye. The suageye have white eyes just like the walleye. The sauger and suageye are smaller than the walleye. Saugers are more likely to be found in large rivers with deep pools but are also found in lakes. The largest sauger caught in South Dakota weighed 7 pounds, 7 ounces.

The walleye got its name because of its white looking eyes. Their eyes collect light, even in low light conditions. This means they can see in the dark. Because they can see in the dark, they mostly feed at night. During the daytime their eyes are very sensitive, so they usually head for deeper water or shady places. Walleye like to live in cooler water and are normally found in the upper part of North America. The current South Dakota state record walleye, weighed 16 pounds, 8 ounces, and was 33 inches long.

Pickerel kind of look like northern pike, but they are not. The Pike is larger in size than the Pickerel. The Pickerel has more spots than the Pike, but the Pike has spots on its fins and pickerel don't. Pickerel has a dark bar beneath their eyes and northern pike don't. Pickerel are also known as gunfish or slime darts. The largest chain pickerel caught in South Dakota is a 9-pound 6-ounce fish.

The Northern Pike is one of the most sought-after fish for anglers. It got its name because it likes to live in cooler water mainly in the northern states of North America. The northern pike is a very aggressive predator. They don't like to live in groups with other fish, they are very territorial and like to live alone. Their behavior is closely affected by weather conditions. The largest Northern Pike caught in South Dakota, weighed 36 pounds and 3 ounces.

The muskellunge called the Musky or Muskie for short is one of the biggest game fish in freshwater lakes. The largest on record was 69 pounds, 15 ounces. The Muskie likes to live in cooler water and can be found in most lakes in the upper part of north America. Anglers look at Muskellunges as trophy fish. They are hard to catch, there's a saying that it takes a thousand casts to catch one. The largest muskellunge caught in South Dakota weighed 40 pounds.

Another breed of the Muskie is the tiger muskie. The tiger muskie is a cross between the northern pike and muskie. They grow larger and faster than normal muskies and northern pikes. The tiger muskie got its name because it has tiger like stripes. Tiger Muskies are very rare and hard to catch. The largest tiger muskellunge caught in South Dakota weighed 37 pounds, 7 ounces.

Fun Facts About South Dakota Fish

1 - The walleye is the official state fish of South Dakota.

2 - South Dakota is home to over 100 fish species, including walleye, northern pike, bluegill, crappie, trout, and others.

3 - The largest fish ever caught in South Dakota, and the state record, is a paddlefish weighing 128 pounds.

4 - Tiger Musky are a hybrid cross between a female muskellunge and a male northern pike.

5 - Salmon were introduced to South Dakota in 2018, and can be caught in Lake Oahe.

6 - The rarest fish in South Dakota is the pallid sturgeon, a federally endangered species, and also the rarest fish in North America.

7 – South Dakota hasrainbow, brown, brook, lake, and splake trout, with the Black Hills being a prime area for these species.

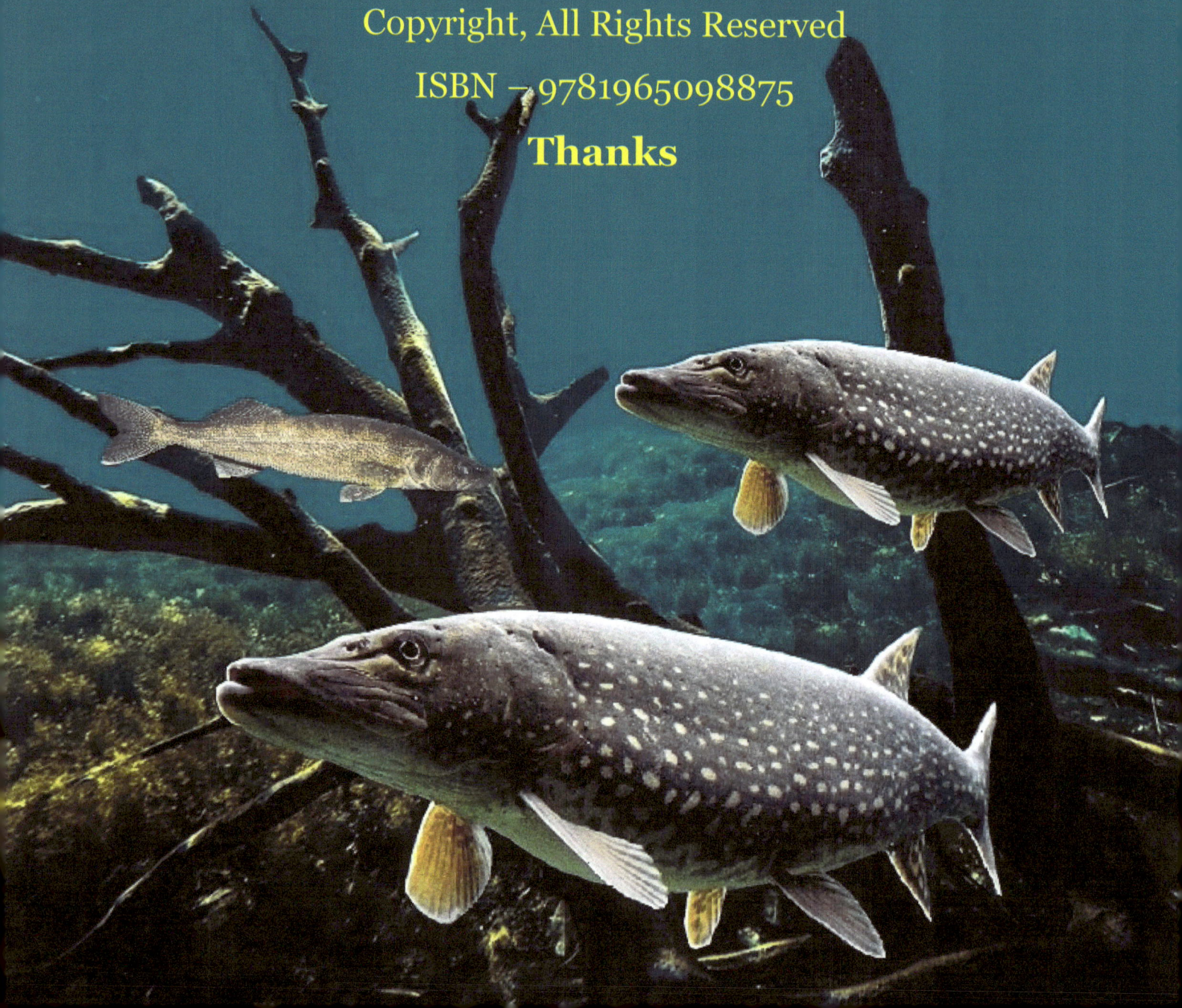

Author Page

Billy Grinslott & Kinsey Marie Books

ISBN – 9781965098875

Thanks